Caramel Fudge Toffee & Brittle

CONFECTIONERY SECRETS

SARA AASUM HULTBERG

PHOTOGRAPHY BY HELÉN PE

weldon**owen**

CONTENTS

Welcome

One of the very first words I said was "dodis," my approximation of *godis*, the Swedish word for candy. By the time I was three years old, I could sit for hours looking through my favorite book about chocolate. It was easy to see what lay in my future.

I have been in the kitchen as long as I can remember, helping my mom, dad, and grandmother with cooking, baking, and desserts. Grandmothers have always spread love and been a model in the kitchen with their joy of cooking and food. When I was quite small, I often experimented with ice cream and various extras that I invited the family to eat, while at the same time I found new recipes for various desserts and baked goods.

In 2014, I won the dream title of "Confectioner of the Year" after having worked for a few years in the United States and Norway. After some months of training and planning, I was the winner! The spring after the contest, I was asked if I would write a book, and of course I wanted to.

Passion for my work only grows, and my biggest incentive is to continually come up with new recipes and test new flavor combinations—and to present them in a lovely way. This is precisely what I was able to do in this book, *Caramel, Fudge, Toffee & Brittle*, which is aimed at both those comfortable in the kitchen and anyone less experienced. The recipes are constructed so that you can easily make them at home in your own kitchen with the equipment and tools you already have.

I love sweets, particularly chocolate, nougat, and toffee. I also love to work with chocolate, especially in combination with salt and vanilla—as you are bound to notice in this book. Keep in mind that the better the ingredients and products you choose, the better the results will be. And be sure to taste—it is as important when you are making candy as when you cook food.

INGREDIENTS

How I Choose
INGREDIENTS

How good your caramels, fudge, toffee, and brittle will be depends on the ingredients. The better their quality, the better the candy will be. It is very important for me to choose good raw materials and that everyone in the production chain should feel good because I bought that ingredient or product. This influences the food industry more than you might believe, and these days there are ever more people conscious about what they eat and why. I also try to select organic products when possible.

Butter

I choose organic butter with an 82 percent fat content.

Sugar

Most often, I use granulated sugar, but sometimes other types of sugar, such as Demerara sugar, muscovado sugar, and confectioners' sugar. In Swedish candy-making we often use liquid glucose, a sugar syrup, but in these recipes honey can be substituted.

In two of the caramel recipes (see pages 26 and 34), I used Swedish dark syrup for a deeper and darker flavor; it contains malt, which complements chocolate. Swedish dark syrup has a very high sugar content (80 percent) from sugar beets. It's available in specialty shops or online, but you can substitute light molasses in any of these recipes. Several recipes use Swedish light syrup; you can substitute Lyle's Golden Syrup here. Sugar and syrup in baking or caramels is used, first of all, to add sweetness but also to make the product longer lasting and to give it a better consistency.

Sugar also helps to intensify other flavors. To get extra flavor without extra sweetness, in some of the recipes, I use, for example, muscovado or Demerara sugar, both of which add an extra caramel tone; you can substitute dark brown sugar, if needed.

Heavy Cream

There are several kinds of cream on the market; I always use organic heavy cream with a 40 percent fat content.

Milk

When a recipe specifies milk, I recommend whole milk. In some recipes, I use sweetened condensed milk. You can find it in cans in any well-stocked grocery.

Chocolate & Cocoa

Valrhona's chocolate is the best, I think, but of course you might want to choose another high-quality chocolate. Personally, I think it is easier to use it in pearl form, because then I don't have to spend time chopping up chocolate; look for chocolate baking pearls in specialty shops or online.

The amount of cocoa and cocoa fat in chocolate is important for the final result. The dark chocolate I use is 66 percent cocoa, and the milk chocolate is 36 percent. My preferred white chocolate is 35 percent cocoa fat.

To get as much cocoa flavor as possible, I use high-quality dark cocoa, preferably Valrhona.

Dried Fruit & Berries

In this book, you will find two kinds of dried fruits and berries: freeze-dried and regular. Freeze-dried berries are crisp and dry and have a crunchy consistency. Regular dried fruit, such as cranberries or blueberries, has a consistency like raisins. You can find either kind of dried fruit in well-stocked groceries and natural foods stores, or online.

Nuts & Seeds

Nuts, almonds, and seeds in these recipes can be substituted with another type if, for example, you are allergic to a particular kind. My favorites are blanched almonds, Marcona almonds, hazelnuts, pistachio nuts, peanuts, pecans, macadamia nuts, and walnuts.

I also like to use kernels and seeds such as sunflower seeds and pine nuts, as well as sesame and poppy seeds.

Eggs

I use large organic eggs. One large egg weighs between 2.2–2.6 ounces (63–73 grams). A large egg white weighs about 1.4 ounces (40 grams).

Vanilla

I always use vanilla beans, but you can substitute vanilla powder. Avoid vanillin, which is a synthetically flavored product.

Little
CONFECTIONERY SCHOOL

Always read through the entire recipe before you start. "Mise en place" translates as "everything in place" in cook's language, and it means that you should plan your baking and cooking well and start by getting out all the ingredients and tools you'll need.

Brown Butter

In some of the recipes, I specify brown butter, as in, for example, Brown Butter Caramels with Sea Salt on page 33. The butter gives a fantastic and nutty flavor; you could say it's the butter, as much as the caramelized sugar, that produces the caramel flavor.

HOW TO MAKE BROWN BUTTER
Melt the butter in a saucepan and let it cook on medium heat until it is dark golden brown and begins to smell nutty. Stir with a whisk so it doesn't burn on the bottom. Remove from the heat as soon as it is ready. Use all of the brown butter, even the dark butter at the bottom.

Caramelized Sugar

Sugar takes on color when it reaches a temperature of about 329°F (165°C). At that point, a chemical reaction takes place, causing the flavor elements of sugar to develop and acquire a buttery taste. And that is precisely what you want to eat. The longer you caramelize sugar, the stronger in taste and darker in color it will be.

HOW TO CARAMELIZE SUGAR
Pour the sugar and water into a saucepan and stir so the ingredients are well blended. Slowly heat the mixture without stirring or whisking; the sugar needs to melt on its own. Shake the pan occasionally so the caramel ingredients will blend. This prevents the sugar from crystallizing or clumping. Let the caramel cook until it takes on color and reaches the temperature or color specified.

On the following pages, you will see how sugar changes color at the various stages of caramelization.

Cooking the Caramel

You need to have patience when you are making caramel, because it takes time—but it's worth every minute! The temperature of the caramel is vitally important so that the finished caramel will have the right consistency. You will need a good digital cooking thermometer so that the mixture can reach the temperature specified in the recipe. The lower the temperature a caramel mixture has, the better it will be, and you will avoid burning the caramel on the bottom of the saucepan.

When you add cold liquid to warm sugar, it will bubble up very rapidly in the saucepan. Always add the liquid one-third at a time and stir between each addition. Be careful, because it will be really hot!

If you don't have a thermometer, you can use a well-proven housewife's method: making a "hard" ball (one that holds together but is pliable) in a cold-water test (see below). Use the temperature recommendation in the recipe as a guideline; it is the temperature I consider will yield the best caramel. You might have another opinion!

If you like soft caramels best, cook to 255°F (124°C); if you prefer a harder caramel, bring the temperature to 259°–260°F (126°–127°C).

HOW TO DO A COLD-WATER TEST
Pour about ½ cup (4 fl oz/125 ml) cold water into a glass and drop in a little bit of caramel. Leave the caramel in for a few seconds and then remove it. Form a little ball between your thumb and forefinger. The ball should hold its shape but still be pliable. If the ball feels too loose, cook the caramel a little longer and then repeat the test.

Toasted Nuts & Seeds

Toasting nuts, coconut, seeds, and kernels before they are used will give the flavor a lift and also add a nice crunch.

HOW TO TOAST NUTS & SEEDS
Heat the oven to 350°F (180°C). Spread the nuts or seeds out on a rimmed baking sheet lined with parchment paper. Toast in the oven for 6–12 minutes, depending on their size. They should smell good and have taken on a nice golden-brown color. Let cool. Toast coconut flakes, sesame seeds, and sunflower seeds in a dry skillet over medium heat, stirring to keep the color even.

Melting Chocolate

The best way to melt chocolate is in a heatproof bowl in the microwave.

HOW TO MELT CHOCOLATE
Chop the chocolate into small pieces or use pearls, and melt them at 10-second intervals at full power on the microwave. Stir between melting intervals until the chocolate is

completely melted. Otherwise, melt it in a heavy saucepan over low heat or in a double boiler over hot water.

Tempering Chocolate

Chocolate is tempered so that it will set properly and not melt at room temperature. Tempering also makes chocolate shiny and gives it a good consistency. Tempering is a little time-consuming and takes a sensitive touch, close attention, and practice. It is very advantageous to have a large marble slab to work on, but a clean counter or rimmed baking sheet will also work. Dark, light, and white chocolate contain different amounts of cocoa fat and need different temperatures for tempering.

HOW TO TEMPER CHOCOLATE

Melt the chocolate (see page 16) and pour three-fourths out onto the work surface. Use an offset spatula or dough scraper to scrape the chocolate back and forth repeatedly while the temperature decreases (see the table to the right). Mix in the remaining fourth of the chocolate when the specified temperature is reached (see Final Temperatures in the table).

Drop a little chocolate onto a saucer to test it. It should firm up rather quickly at room temperature and have a shiny surface. If it seems too warm, you can pour one-fourth of the chocolate onto the work surface and scrape it back and forth until the temperature lowers; mix in the rest of the chocolate.

IMPORTANT
CHOCOLATE
TEMPERATURES

For Melting:
Dark:
113°–122°F
(45°–50°C)
Light:
113°F (45°C)
White:
104°–113°F
(40°–45°C)

*On the
Work Surface:*
Dark:
84°F (29°C)
Light:
82°F (28°C)
White:
80°F (27°C)

*Final
Temperatures:*
Dark:
87°–89°F
(31°–32°C)
Light:
86°–87°F
(30°–31°C)
White:
84°–86°F
(29°–30°C)

Dipping in Chocolate

If you put caramel, berries, or something else you want to dip in chocolate in the freezer for about 20 minutes to chill, then you won't need to temper the chocolate.

HOW TO DIP IN CHOCOLATE

Melt the chocolate (see page 16) and let it cool to about 104°F (40°C). Take the pieces to be dipped out of the freezer and dip them one by one into the chocolate. Wipe away any excess from the bottom of the pieces using parchment paper. Lay the dipped pieces on parchment paper and leave until the chocolate has set.

Everything in Its Own Time

I usually let candy stand at room temperature for at least 6 hours before serving so it will have a good consistency.

Cutting Candy into Pieces

Use a very sharp and clean knife. Rinse the knife under boiling water and then dry it. Cut away any uneven edges so that all the pieces will be the same size.

Storing & Serving

Store candy in a cool place in an airtight container. Chocolate is best if kept at a temperature of about 65°F (18°C).

GOOD TOOLS

Make sure you always use clean and dry tools.

These are my favorite tools for successful candy-making in the kitchen.

Heavy Saucepan

Use a low and wide saucepan rather than a small and high one, and one that is too large rather than too small. Caramel can easily boil over in a saucepan if it is too small. The pan should also have a somewhat heavy bottom.

Stand Mixer

If you are making, for example, a French nougat (see page 47), which needs a long whisking time, the results will be better if you use a stand mixer.

Scale & Thermometer

A kitchen scale and a digital cooking thermometer are good investments.

Heatproof Spatula

A good silicone spatula that can take heat up to 480°F (250°C) can be used in both bowls and saucepans.

Balloon Whisk

Make sure that your balloon whisk can tolerate high heat. These days, balloon whisks are made of silicone and can be used at temperatures up to 480°F (250°C). An ordinary stainless-steel whisk works just as well.

Pans

Most of the recipes in this book make enough to fill a baking pan 8 x 8 inches (20 x 20 cm) in diameter. I think that's a good size for a small amount of caramel, nougat, or brittle to make at home. If you want to make more and double the recipe, you will, of course, need a larger pan.

Silicone Mats & Parchment Paper

Silicone (Silpat) mats prevent sticking more effectively than parchment paper. You can buy silicone mats in well-stocked kitchen supply shops or department stores. Of course, you can also use parchment paper.

Recipes

SALTED CARAMELS
with TOASTED COCONUT

I often make these caramels at home; they are more festive when wrapped in waxed paper or cellophane. Toasted coconut and caramel always combine well, and sea salt gives them that little bit extra.

MAKES ABOUT
20 CARAMELS

1 cup (8 fl oz/250 ml) heavy cream

7 tablespoons (3½ oz/105 g) butter

1¼ cups (10 oz/315 g) sugar

⅔ cup (5 fl oz/160 ml) liquid glucose or honey

⅓ cup (3 fl oz/80 ml) water

¾ cup (2 oz/60 g) toasted coconut flakes

½ teaspoon sea salt

Heat the cream and butter in a saucepan. Remove from the heat when the butter has melted. At the same time, in another saucepan, bring the sugar, glucose, and water to a boil over medium heat until it reaches a temperature of 374°–392°F (190°–200°C) and is dark golden brown. (See Caramelized Sugar on pages 13–15.)

One-third at a time, pour the cream mixture into the sugar syrup. Mix with a whisk between each addition. Bring the caramel back to a boil and cook until 255°F (124°C), or hard-ball stage (see page 16 for how to do a cold-water test). Stir in the coconut and sea salt.

Line a pan about 8 x 8 inches (20 x 20 cm) with parchment paper. Pour in the caramel and leave at room temperature for at least 6 hours to set.

Cut the caramel into pieces.

If you want to bring out the most flavor in coconut, toast it!

CHOCOLATE CARAMELS with COCOA NIBS

This is the ultimate caramel, or at least I (with a weakness for dark chocolate) think so. The slightly bitter cocoa nibs complement the sweetness of the caramel and add a delightful crunch. You can find cocoa nibs in well-stocked groceries.

MAKES ABOUT 16 LARGE CARAMELS

3¹/₂ oz (105 g) dark chocolate

7 tablespoons (3¹/₂ oz/105 g) butter

1 vanilla bean

³/₄ cup (6 fl oz/180 ml) heavy cream

1¹/₄ cups (10¹/₂ oz/315 g) sugar

¹/₃ cup (3 fl oz/80 ml) Swedish dark syrup or light molasses

Pinch of sea salt

2 tablespoons cocoa nibs

Chop the chocolate.

Melt the butter in a saucepan on low heat. Cut the vanilla bean in half lengthwise and scrape out the seeds into the saucepan. Add the cream, sugar, syrup, chocolate, and salt. Stir well.

On medium heat, cook the caramel for about 30 minutes until it begins to thicken and then continue cooking until it reaches 255°F (124°C), or hard-ball stage (see page 16 for how to do a cold-water test). Stir occasionally.

Line a pan about 8 x 8 inches (20 x 20 cm) with parchment paper. Pour the caramel into the lined pan and sprinkle with the cocoa nibs. Leave at room temperature for at least 6 hours to set.

Cut the caramel into squares.

For a slightly sweeter caramel, substitute milk chocolate for the dark chocolate.

CARAMELS with TOASTED SESAME SEEDS, POPPY SEEDS & LEMON

When I was small, I often ate little sesame seed cakes made with caramelized sugar and sesame seeds. Ever since then, sesame seeds and caramel have been my favorite combination. Here, I've made caramels with sesame and poppy seeds plus lemon. The acidity from the lemon perfectly balances the sweet caramel and nuttiness of the seeds. It's a more adult caramel.

MAKES ABOUT 14 CARAMELS

1 cup (8 fl oz/250 ml) heavy cream

7 tablespoons (3½ oz/105 g) butter

1¼ cups (10 oz/315 g) sugar

⅓ cup (3 fl oz/80 ml) liquid glucose or honey

⅓ cup (3 fl oz/80 ml) water

Grated zest and juice of 1 lemon

¾ cup (3 oz/90 g) toasted sesame seeds

4 tablespoons (2 oz/60 g) poppy seeds

1 teaspoon sea salt

Heat the cream and butter in a saucepan. Remove from the heat when the butter is completely melted. At the same time, in another saucepan, mix the sugar, glucose, and water. Bring to a boil over medium heat. Cook until the mixture reaches a temperature of 374°–392°F (190°–200°C) and is a rather dark golden brown (see Caramelized Sugar on pages 13–15).

One-third at a time, pour the cream mixture into the sugar syrup. Mix with a whisk between each addition. Add the lemon zest and lemon juice and cook until the mixture reaches 255°F (124°C), or hard-ball stage (see page 16 for how to do a cold-water test). Stir occasionally. Mix in the sesame seeds, 2 tablespoons of the poppy seeds, and the salt.

Line a pan about 8 x 8 inches (20 x 20 cm) with parchment paper. Pour in the caramel and sprinkle with the remaining 2 tablespoons poppy seeds. Leave at room temperature for at least 6 hours to set.

Cut the caramel into small pieces.

RASPBERRY CARAMELS DIPPED in WHITE CHOCOLATE

If you want caramels that aren't so chewy and are fresher tasting, then try these. Raspberry and caramel make a great combination. The crunchy freeze-dried raspberries contrast with the stickiness of the caramel.

MAKES ABOUT 14 CARAMELS

About 2 cups (8 oz/250 g) fresh or frozen raspberries

¾ cup (6 fl oz/180 ml) heavy cream

3 tablespoons butter

1¼ cups (10 oz/315 g) sugar

⅓ cup (3 fl oz/80 ml) liquid glucose or honey

⅓ cup (3 fl oz/80 ml) water

7 oz (220 g) white chocolate

⅓ cup (⅓ oz/10 g) freeze-dried raspberries

These caramels will taste best with fresh raspberries, but if you can't find them, frozen raspberries are almost as good.

Process the fresh or frozen raspberries in a blender and pass through a fine-mesh sieve to make 1 cup (8 fl oz/250 ml) purée. Mix the purée with the cream and butter in a saucepan and heat on low until the butter melts.

Mix the sugar, glucose, and water in another saucepan and bring to a boil; continue to cook until the mixture reaches about 320°F (160°C) and has just changed color (see Caramelized Sugar on pages 13–15). One-third at a time, pour the cream mixture into the sugar syrup. Mix with a whisk between each addition.

On medium heat, cook until mixture reaches 255°F (124°C), or hard-ball stage (see page 16 for how to do a cold-water test). Stir occasionally.

Line a pan about 8 x 8 inches (20 x 20 cm) with parchment paper. Pour in the caramel. Let set at room temperature for at least 6 hours.

Cut the caramel into rectangles. Melt or temper the chocolate (see pages 16–17). Dip half of each caramel in the chocolate. Wipe the excess chocolate from the bottom and place the pieces on parchment paper. Sprinkle the caramels with the freeze-dried raspberries.

BROWN BUTTER CARAMELS with SEA SALT

I think brown butter goes with almost anything, and it gives these caramels a characteristic flavor and nuttiness. These rich butter caramels will definitely be a hit with anyone you share them with!

MAKES ABOUT 25 CARAMELS

- 1/2 cup plus 6 tablespoons (14 oz/440 g) butter
- ¾ cup (6 fl oz/180 ml) heavy cream
- ¾ cup (6 oz/185 g) Demerara or dark brown sugar
- ¾ cup (6 oz/185 g) granulated sugar
- 1/3 cup (3 fl oz/80 ml) liquid glucose or honey
- ¼ cup (2 fl oz/60 ml) water
- 1 teaspoon sea salt

Don't be too cautious with the brown butter; for extra-tasty caramels, it should brown just to the point of being too dark.

Brown the butter in a saucepan (see Brown Butter on page 13). Blend in the cream and Demerara sugar and set the pan aside.

Mix the granulated sugar, honey, and water in another saucepan. Bring to a boil and cook until the mixture changes color and takes on a dark tone (see Caramelized Sugar on pages 13–15).

One-third at a time, pour the cream mixture into the sugar syrup. Mix with a whisk between each addition. Cook until the mixture reaches 255°F (124°C), or hard-ball stage (see page 16 for how to do a cold-water test). Stir occasionally.

Line a pan about 9 x 12 inches (25 x 30 cm) with parchment paper. Pour in a thin layer of caramel. Sprinkle with the sea salt and leave at room temperature for at least 6 hours to set.

Cut the caramel into pieces.

CHOCOLATE CARAMELS
~with~ MINT SUGAR

Mint adds an extra freshness to these caramels, which are dipped in dark chocolate and topped with mint sugar. If you are ambitious and have extra time, the caramels will be best if you temper the chocolate; see page 17.

MAKES ABOUT 16 CARAMELS

3/4 cup (6 fl oz/180 ml)
    heavy cream

1¼ cups (10 oz/315 g) sugar

1/3 cup (1/3 oz/10 g) loosely
    packed fresh mint leaves

1/3 cup (3 fl oz/80 ml) Swedish
    dark syrup or light molasses

7 tablespoons (3½ oz/105 g)
    butter

1/4 cup (3/4 oz/20 g)
    unsweetened cocoa powder

12 oz (375 g) dark chocolate

MINT SUGAR

1/4 cup (1/4 oz/7 g) loosely
    packed fresh mint leaves

1/3 cup (2½ oz/75 g) sugar

Heat the cream in a saucepan with 1/4 cup (2 oz/60 g) of the sugar and the 1/3 cup (1/3 oz/10 g) mint leaves. Set aside and let steep for about 30 minutes.

Taste the cream mixture to be sure it has a good minty flavor. Sieve out the leaves and add the syrup, butter, cocoa, and the remaining 1 cup (8 oz/250 g) sugar to the cream mixture. On medium heat, bring the mixture to a boil and cook until it reaches 255°F (124°C), or hard-ball stage (see page 16 for how to do a cold-water test). Stir occasionally.

Line a pan about 8 x 8 inches (20 x 20 cm) with parchment paper. Pour in the caramel and leave at room temperature for at least 6 hours to set.

Cut the caramel into pieces. Melt or temper the chocolate (see pages 16–17). In a blender, process the mint leaves and sugar for the mint sugar topping.

Dip the caramels in the melted chocolate using a fork. Place the caramels on parchment paper and sprinkle with the mint sugar.

LICORICE CARAMELS
with LIME & SEA SALT

Many people love the flavor of licorice, and not just in sweets but in other foods as well. For these caramels, I use lime to reach a fine balance between the licorice and the caramel. I like to add flaky sea salt for its look and to intensify the flavors.

MAKES ABOUT 24 CARAMELS

¾ cup (6 oz/185 g) butter

1 cup (8 fl oz/250 ml) heavy cream

1¼ cups (10 oz/315 g) sugar

⅓ cup (3 fl oz/80 ml) liquid glucose or honey

⅓ cup (3 fl oz/80 ml) water

¼ cup (2 fl oz/60 ml) licorice syrup

2 teaspoons licorice powder

Grated zest of 1 lime

1 tablespoon fresh-squeezed lime juice

1 teaspoon flaky sea salt

You can find licorice powder (also called granulated licorice) and licorice syrup in specialty foods stores, natural foods stores, or online.

Melt the butter with the cream in a saucepan. In another saucepan, mix the sugar, glucose, and water. Bring to a boil and cook, without stirring, until the mixture reaches a temperature of 338°F (170°C) and has taken on a golden brown color (see Caramelized Sugar on pages 13–15).

One-third at a time, pour the cream mixture into the sugar syrup. Mix with a whisk between each addition. Bring back to a boil and then add the licorice syrup, 1 teaspoon of the licorice powder, the lime zest and juice, and ½ teaspoon of the salt. Cook until the mixture reaches 255°F (124°C), or hard-ball stage (see page 16 for how to do a cold-water test). Remove from the heat and let cool for a couple of minutes.

Pour the caramel onto parchment paper and sprinkle with the remaining ½ teaspoon salt and the remaining 1 teaspoon licorice powder. Leave at room temperature for at least 6 hours to set.

Cut or break the caramel into pieces.

CHOCOLATE ~or~ VANILLA FUDGE

Caramels and toffee have a firmer consistency and are cooked to a higher temperature than fudge. Fudge has a softer consistency because the sugar crystallizes as the mixture cools due to constant stirring.

MAKES ABOUT 24 PIECES
EACH

CHOCOLATE FUDGE

1 vanilla bean

1¼ cups (10 oz/315 g) sugar

1 cup (8 fl oz/250 ml)
  heavy cream

⅓ cup (3 fl oz/80 ml) milk

⅓ cup (3 fl oz/180 ml)
  Swedish dark syrup or
  light molasses

¼ cup (2 oz/60 g) butter

3½ oz (105 g) dark chocolate

VANILLA FUDGE

1 vanilla bean

1¾ cups (14 oz/440 g) sugar

¾ cup (6 fl oz/180 ml)
  heavy cream

¾ cup (6 fl oz/180 ml) milk

½ cup (4 fl oz/125 ml)
  Swedish dark syrup or
  light molasses

¼ cup (2 oz/60 g) butter

⅛ teaspoon salt

CHOCOLATE FUDGE

Line a pan about 8 x 12 inches (20 x 30 cm) with parchment paper.

Cut the vanilla bean in half lengthwise and scrape out the seeds into a saucepan. Add the sugar, cream, milk, syrup, and butter. Heat on low until the butter melts. Stir occasionally with a heatproof spatula.

Raise the heat to medium and cook the mixture until it reaches 242°F (117°C). Remove from the heat and let cool for awhile.

Chop the chocolate and add it to the mixture. Stir with a heatproof spatula until the mixture thickens and cools to about 158°F (70°C), making sure that it doesn't become grainy. Now it's ready.

Pour the fudge into the prepared pan and leave at room temperature for at least 6 hours to set. Cut into squares.

VANILLA FUDGE

Make as for chocolate fudge until the mixture reaches 242°F (117°C). Remove from the heat and let the bubbling subside for a while. Stir with a heatproof spatula until the mixture thickens, is no longer glossy, and has cooled to 131°–140°F (55°–60°C).

Pour the fudge into the prepared pan and leave at room temperature for at least 6 hours to set. Cut into squares.

Fudge is made with cream
and milk, so it has
a lower fat content
than caramels.

S'MORES FUDGE

These tasty sweets were inspired by an American dessert, s'mores: fire-toasted marshmallows with chocolate between two graham crackers. The name derives from "some more," which you'll understand once you've eaten some. There are few ingredients, no temperature to watch, and they are soooooo good!

MAKES ABOUT 24 PIECES

- 2 cups (3½ oz/105 g) mini-marshmallows
- 5 graham crackers
- 7 oz (220 g) dark chocolate
- 7 oz (220 g) milk chocolate
- 2 tablespoons butter
- 14-oz (400-g) can sweetened condensed milk

Preheat the oven to 350°F (180°C). "Toast" half of the marshmallows on a rimmed baking sheet lined with parchment paper for 4–5 minutes, until they are golden brown and have a crispy surface. Coarsely crush the crackers. Chop the two chocolates and dice the butter.

Heat the condensed milk in a saucepan on low heat. Add the chocolates and butter and quickly blend together with a heatproof spatula. Melt the chocolates and butter until the mixture is smooth and even. Stir in the crackers and most of the marshmallows (toasted and untoasted), saving some marshmallows for the topping.

Scrape the mixture into a pan about 8 x 12 inches (20 x 30 cm). Cover and refrigerate for at least 6 hours to set. Cut the fudge into pieces.

DARK CHOCOLATE FUDGE with FIGS & PISTACHIOS

If you are lucky enough to find pistachios as pretty as those shown here, then you can make some fantastic fudge. The nuts combined with figs produce a smooth fudge with a great consistency. If you can't find shelled green pistachios, you can substitute regular unsalted pistachios with a thin rosy skin.

MAKES ABOUT 25 PIECES

5½ oz (170 g) dried figs

15 oz (470 g) dark chocolate

2 tablespoons butter

14-oz (400-g) can sweetened condensed milk

1¼ cups (5 oz/155 g) shelled pistachios

Cut the figs into small pieces. Chop the chocolate and dice the butter.

On low, heat the sweetened condensed milk in a saucepan. Add the chocolate and butter and mix quickly with a heatproof spatula. Melt the chocolate and butter completely so the mixture will be smooth and even.

Set aside a handful of pistachios for garnish and then fold the rest into the fudge with the figs. Scrape into a pan about 8 x 12 inches (20 x 30 cm).

Sprinkle the remaining pistachios over the fudge and cover the pan with plastic wrap. Refrigerate for at least 6 hours to set.

Cut the fudge into pieces.

FUDGE with LIME, WHITE CHOCOLATE & BLUEBERRIES

White chocolate has fat only from cocoa beans and is much sweeter than dark and milk chocolate. For that reason, it blends well with tart ingredients such as citrus or passion fruit. This tasty fudge incorporates lime and blueberries.

MAKES ABOUT 25 PIECES

1 vanilla bean

1 cup (8 oz/250 g) sugar

1 cup (8 fl oz/250 ml) heavy cream

⅓ cup (3 fl oz/80 ml) milk

⅓ cup (3 fl oz/80 ml) Swedish light syrup or Lyle's Golden Syrup

3½ oz (105 g) white chocolate

¼ cup (2 oz/60 g) butter

Grated zest of 3 limes

Juice of 1 lime

⅓ cup (2 oz/60 g) dried blueberries

Dried blueberries have the same texture as raisins and work perfectly here.

Line the bottom of an 8 x 8-inch (20 x 20-cm) pan with parchment paper.

Cut the vanilla bean in half lengthwise and scrape the seeds into a saucepan. Add the sugar, cream, milk, and syrup. Heat the mixture on low until the butter has melted. Stir occasionally with a heatproof spatula.

Raise the heat to medium and cook until the mixture reaches 242°F (117°C). Remove from the heat and let cool for a while.

Chop the chocolate and dice the butter. Mix the chocolate and butter, two-thirds of the lime zest, and the lime juice into the saucepan. Stir constantly until the fudge has cooled to about 158°F (70°C) and loses its gloss. Make sure it doesn't become grainy.

Pour the fudge into the prepared pan, sprinkle on the remaining lime zest, and top with the dried blueberries. Leave at room temperature for at least 6 hours to set.

Cut into squares.

FRENCH NOUGAT MONTÉLIMAR

I promise, there is not much that beats fresh Montélimar nougat! The nougat you make yourself will be one hundred times better than store-bought. The base is actually a meringue whipped with a hot sugar-and-honey syrup. Give some away in a lovely bowl wrapped with cellophane—the perfect present.

MAKES 10–12 PIECES

1¼ cups (10 oz/315 g) granulated sugar

⅔ cup (5 fl oz/160 ml) honey

¼ cup (2 fl oz/60 ml) liquid glucose or honey

⅓ cup (3 fl oz/80 ml) water

2 large egg whites

12 oz (375 g) mixed toasted nuts, such as Marcona almonds, hazelnuts, and pistachios

⅓ cup (1½ oz/45 g) confectioners' sugar

Mix 1 cup (8 oz/250 g) of the granulated sugar with the honey, glucose, and water in a saucepan and bring to a boil over low heat to make a sugar syrup. When the syrup reaches about 266°F (130°C), whisk the egg whites until foamy in a bowl. Add the remaining ¼ cup (2 oz/60 g) granulated sugar and continue whisking until the whites form stiff, glossy peaks.

Continue to boil the sugar syrup until it reaches 302°F (150°C). Pour the syrup in a thin stream into the bowl and whisk until the meringue is firm but still lukewarm. Stir in the nuts.

Line a 6-cup (48–fl oz/1.5-l) bowl with parchment paper. Sift some confectioners' sugar over the paper to coat it evenly.

Dip a rubber spatula in oil so the nougat won't stick and transfer the nougat to the bowl. Lightly press it down and dust it with more confectioners' sugar. Leave at room temperature for at least 6 hours to set.

Cut the nougat into wedges.

You can read more about making French nougat on the next page...

Sara's
NOUGAT CLASS

There are many different types of nougat, and I've included recipes for both hard and soft nougat in this book. Soft nougat is common in Italy, Spain, and France, but various regions in each of these countries have their own special versions.

French nougat Montélimar (page 47) has a base of egg whites, honey, and sugar and usually contains almonds. I decided to try a little mixture of nuts here: pistachios, Marcona almonds, and hazelnuts. The pistachios add a lovely green color, and the hazelnuts contribute extra flavor. For even more flavor, I toast the nuts and almonds first.

A soft nougat like this one is made the same way as an Italian nougat. You begin by whisking a light meringue with egg whites and sugar and cooking a sugar syrup with sugar, honey, liquid glucose, and water until it reaches 302°F (150°C). It is important to handle the sugar syrup very carefully, as it is extremely hot.

With this type of nougat, it is almost a necessity to have a food processor or a stand mixer (such as a KitchenAid) that holds a stainless-steel bowl firmly in place while you whisk. As soon as you have whisked the meringue mixture and the sugar syrup has heated to the correct temperature, reduce the speed of the mixer and slowly pour in the syrup in a thin stream. Increase the speed again and whisk until the temperature has dropped and the meringue has a firm consistency.

"SNICKERS"
with Nougat, Peanuts, Caramel & Chocolate

After my time in New York, I wanted to have nuts and, most of all, peanuts, in absolutely everything. The best combination I can imagine is peanuts, chocolate, and caramel. This is one of my favorite recipes; it is both easy and fun to make at home. And it really does taste almost like Snickers candy bars!

MAKES ABOUT 18 PIECES

NOUGAT

¾ cup (6 oz/185 g) plus 2 tablespoons granulated sugar

⅓ cup (3 fl oz/80 ml) honey

⅓ cup (3 fl oz/80 ml) liquid glucose

⅓ cup (3 fl oz/80 ml) water

2 small or 1½ large egg whites (2 oz/60 g)

3 tablespoons confectioners' sugar for dusting

CARAMEL

½ vanilla bean

⅔ cup (5 oz/155 g) granulated sugar

¼ cup (2 fl oz/60 ml) liquid glucose or honey

⅓ cup (3 fl oz/80 ml) heavy cream

3½ tablespoons (1½ oz/45 g) butter

⅔ cup (3 oz/90 g) salted peanuts

PEANUT GANACHE

3½ ounces (105 g) dark chocolate

1¾ ounces (50 g) milk chocolate

1 tablespoon peanut butter

½ cup (4 fl oz/125 ml) heavy cream

1 tablespoon honey

For the nougat, mix the ¾ cup (6 oz/185 g) granulated sugar, the honey, glucose, and water in a saucepan and bring to a boil to make a sugar syrup. When the syrup reaches about 266°F (130°C), begin whisking the egg whites in a separate bowl. Add the 2 tablespoons granulated sugar a little at a time to form a meringue with stiff, glossy peaks.

When the sugar syrup reaches 302°F (150°C), pour it in a thin stream into the meringue. Whisk until the meringue is firm and lukewarm.

Line a pan about 8 x 8 inches (20 x 20 cm) with parchment paper. Sift some of the confectioners' sugar over the paper to coat it.

Dip a spatula in oil so the nougat won't stick and transfer the nougat to the lined pan. Dust with more confectioners' sugar and press the nougat into the pan.

For the caramel, cut the vanilla bean in half lengthwise and scrape the seeds into a saucepan. Mix in the sugar, glucose, cream, and butter. Heat on low until the butter has melted. Increase the heat to medium and cook until the caramel reaches 253°F (123°C). Remove the pan from the heat and pour the caramel over the nougat. Sprinkle on the peanuts and let the caramel set at room temperature for a while.

For the ganache, chop the dark and milk chocolates. Put the chocolates and peanut butter in a bowl.

Heat the cream with the honey in a saucepan. Pour the warm cream over the chocolate and peanut butter. Stir with a heatproof spatula until the mixture is a smooth ganache.

Pour the ganache over the caramel layer in the pan and leave at room temperature for at least 6 hours to set. Cut into pieces.

Heat a sharp knife in hot water for a bit and then dry off the water. It is easier to cut candy into clean pieces with a warm knife.

PEANUT NOUGAT
Peanut Butter Cups

When you caramelize nuts, process them into a praline, and then mix that with chocolate, you will have nougat. This easy candy reminds me of American peanut butter cups. This is my version!

MAKES ABOUT 25 PIECES

⅓ cup (2½ oz/75 g) sugar

1 cup (5 oz/155 g) salted peanuts

8 oz (250 g) milk chocolate

Pinch of fine salt

Over medium heat, melt the sugar in a saucepan until it caramelizes and takes on a golden brown color (see Caramelized Sugar, pages 13–15). Pour the caramel onto a baking sheet lined with parchment paper and let set.

Break the caramel into small pieces and process them with the peanuts to a very fine mixture.

Chop the chocolate and melt it (see page 16). Mix the chocolate with the peanuts and caramel. Add the salt.

Fill a pastry bag with the nougat and pipe it into mini muffin pans—this is the easiest way to shape the candy. If you don't have a pastry bag, you can fill the muffin pans using a small spoon. Leave until set.

You can also make peanut nougat as a brittle. Just pour the nougat into a pan and let set. Break the brittle into pieces.

WHEY TRUFFLES with ALMONDS

Besides the cream and butter I often use in my recipes, I also like to use whey powder, also called whey protein powder. It provides a perfect sweet and salt combination that is an excellent pairing with dark chocolate. Marcona almonds originally came from Spain and are considered the finest of all almonds.

MAKES ABOUT 12 PIECES

1/3 cup (3 fl oz/80 ml) water

2 1/2 teaspoons fine salt

3/4 cup (3 oz/90 g) blanched almonds, preferably Marcona almonds

12 oz (375 g) dark chocolate

2 tablespoons butter

2/3 cup (5 fl oz/160 ml) heavy cream

2 cups (5 1/2 oz/170 g) soft whey butter

Why not gift these fine truffles in the pan?

Preheat the oven to 350°F (180°C). Mix the water and salt in a saucepan and bring to a boil over high heat. Add the almonds and reduce the heat to medium. Stir until all the water has evaporated and the almonds are white with the salt. Spread the almonds on a rimmed baking sheet lined with parchment paper and toast in the oven for about 10 minutes; remove from oven and let cool.

Chop the dark chocolate finely and pour into a bowl. Dice the butter.

Stir the cream and whey butter together and heat the mixture in a saucepan. Pour the mixture over the chocolate. Add the butter and stir until the mixture is smooth and even.

Line a round pan about 8 inches (20 cm) in diameter with parchment paper and pour in the truffle mixture. Spread it evenly in the pan and then sprinkle the toasted almonds on top. Leave at room temperature for at least 6 hours to set.

Cut into pieces.

ORANGE CHOCOLATE TRUFFLES DIPPED IN CHOCOLATE & COCOA

People seem to either love the combination of chocolate and orange or despise it. I'm a person who likes it! Here is my recipe for super-good truffles with chocolate and orange.

MAKES ABOUT 25 TRUFFLES

3½ ounces (105 g) dark chocolate, plus 5½ oz (170 g) dark chocolate for dipping

7 ounces (220 g) milk chocolate

2 tablespoons butter

½ vanilla bean

½ cup (4 fl oz/125 ml) heavy cream

2 teaspoons honey

1 teaspoon grated orange zest

1 tablespoon fresh squeezed orange juice

¾ cup (2 oz/60 g) unsweetened cocoa powder

You can use either blood oranges or regular oranges for these truffles.

Chop the 3½ ounces (105 g) dark chocolate and the milk chocolate and put in a bowl. Dice the butter.

Cut the vanilla bean in half lengthwise and scrape the seeds into a saucepan. Add the cream, honey, orange zest, and orange juice; bring to a boil. Pour the mixture over the chocolate in the bowl and stir until it has melted.

Mix in the diced butter and let it melt. Stir until smooth.

Line a pan about 8 x 8 inches (20 x 20 cm) with parchment paper. Pour in the truffle mixture and refrigerate for at least 3 hours to set.

Cut the truffle mixture into small pieces about ¾ inch (2 cm) square.

Melt or temper the 5½ ounces (170 g) dark chocolate for dipping the truffles (see pages 16–17). Leave it to cool for a while. Pour the cocoa into a deep platter.

Using a fork, dip the truffles one by one into the cocoa so that each piece is evenly coated on all sides. Leave to set. Shake off any excess cocoa to serve.

WHITE CHOCOLATE TRUFFLES
with PASSION FRUIT

Truffles can be varied endlessly! Here is a refreshing version. Fresh passion fruit adds a lovely flavor to a very creamy white chocolate truffle. Dream yourself into the Caribbean by rolling the truffles in toasted coconut instead.

MAKES ABOUT 30 TRUFFLES

8 oz (250 g) white chocolate, chopped

2 tablespoons butter, diced

3 passion fruits

½ cup (4 fl oz/125 ml) heavy cream

1 tablespoon liquid glucose or honey

¾ cup (3 oz/90 g) confectioners' sugar

Put the chocolate and butter in a saucepan.

Scoop the meat of the passion fruits out of the skins and into another saucepan. Pour in the cream and glucose. Bring to a boil. Using the back of a large spoon, press the juice from the fruit pulp through a fine-mesh sieve into the chocolate and butter.

Melt the chocolate mixture over medium-low heat. Using a heatproof spatula, fold the mixture together to make a smooth cream; you can use an immersion blender if necessary.

Scrape the mixture into a bowl and cover with plastic wrap pressed directly onto the surface of the truffle mixture. Leave the bowl at room temperature for at least 6 hours to set. (When the truffles set at room temperature, they are easier to shape.)

Shape the truffles into small eggs, using a little spoon that you dip in warm water and dry between each egg.

Sift the confectioners' sugar into a deep platter. Roll the truffles in the sugar, coating them evenly.

MILK CHOCOLATE TRUFFLES *with* CARAMELIZED NUTS

Macadamias are one of my favorite nuts. They have a little more fat and a lower protein content than, for example, almonds and cashews. Macadamias are also a little more expensive than other nuts, but try them anyway. They combine very well with the milk chocolate, honey, and salt in this recipe.

MAKES ABOUT 35 TRUFFLES

CARAMELIZED NUTS

7 oz (220 g) roasted
  macadamia nuts

¼ cup (2 fl oz/60 ml) honey

½ teaspoon fine salt

14 oz (440 g) milk chocolate

¼ cup (2 oz/60 g) butter

¾ cup (6 fl oz/180 ml)
  heavy cream

2 tablespoons honey

To make the caramelized nuts, preheat the oven to 350°F (180°C). Coarsely chop the nuts. Mix them with the honey and salt in a bowl and then spread them out on a rimmed baking sheet lined with parchment paper. Toast in the oven for about 8 minutes; remove from the oven and let cool.

Coarsely chop the milk chocolate. Cut the butter into small pieces. Put the chocolate and butter in a bowl.

Mix the cream and honey in a saucepan, bring the mixture to a boil, and then pour over the chocolate mixture. Stir the mixture with a spatula until smooth; process with an immersion blender if necessary. Cover with plastic wrap pressed directly onto the surface of the truffle mixture and leave at room temperature for at least 6 hours to set.

Process the caramelized nuts in a blender until finely chopped. Pour the nuts out on a plate.

Roll the truffles into balls and then roll the balls into the nuts, coating them evenly.

DARK CHOCOLATE TRUFFLES
with RUM

A really good dark chocolate truffle always goes well with coffee. These have dark rum, which pairs well with espresso and a good after-dinner drink. Decide if you want to dip the truffles in cocoa or confectioners' sugar. Or, why not half and half, for more effect?

MAKES ABOUT 35 TRUFFLES

9 oz (280 g) dark chocolate

¹⁄₄ cup (2 oz/60 g) butter

³⁄₄ cup (6 fl oz/180 ml) heavy cream

2 tablespoons honey

2 tablespoons dark rum

³⁄₄ cup (2 oz/60 g) unsweetened cocoa powder or ³⁄₄ cup (3 oz/90 g) confectioners' sugar, or ¹⁄₃ cup (1 oz/90 g) cocoa and ¹⁄₃ cup (1¹⁄₂ oz/ 45 g) confectioners' sugar

Coarsely chop the chocolate and place in a bowl. Dice the butter.

Mix the cream and honey in a saucepan and bring to a boil. Remove from the heat as soon as the cream begins to boil; pour over the chocolate.

Let the chocolate melt for a few minutes and then stir with a heatproof spatula until all the chocolate has melted. Add the butter and stir until it has melted. Finally, add the rum in a thin stream while you stir with the spatula until the truffle mixture is even and smooth.

Cover with plastic wrap pressed directly onto the surface of the truffle mixture. Leave at room temperature for at least 6 hours to set.

Sift the cocoa or confectioners' sugar (or each separately) and pour into a deep platter (or two platters). Roll the truffles into balls. Roll the truffles in the cocoa or confectioners' sugar, coating them evenly.

CLASSIC TOFFEE
That's Not So Classic

Quickly losing all patience when trying to pour toffee into little paper cups is a situation that many are familiar with. The trouble with the cups is that they easily overturn, so that toffee goes all over the kitchen. Why make it difficult for yourself? I used a bread pan for this toffee and then cut it into long pieces—simple but just as good.

MAKES ABOUT
30 LARGE PIECES

1/3 cup (2 1/2 oz/75 g) Demerara or dark brown sugar

1/3 cup (3 oz/90 g) granulated sugar

3/4 cup (6 fl oz/180 ml) heavy cream

3/4 cup (6 fl oz/180 ml) Swedish light syrup or Lyle's Golden Syrup

3/4 cup (3 oz/90 g) blanched almonds, preferably Marcona almonds

3/4 cup (3 oz/90 g) walnuts

Combine the Demerara and granulated sugars, cream, and syrup in a saucepan; bring to a boil over medium heat and cook for 20–30 minutes, stirring occasionally.

When the toffee reaches 255°F (124°C°), or hard-ball stage (see page 16 for how to do a cold-water test), remove the pan from the heat and mix in the almonds and walnuts.

Line the bottom of a 6-cup (48–fl oz/1.5-l) bread pan with parchment paper and pour in the toffee. Leave at room temperature for at least 6 hours to set.

Cut the toffee into pieces.

To easily cut the toffee, use a really sharp knife heated in hot water.

HONEY TOFFEE *with* PISTACHIOS & LEMON

Green pistachio nuts in place of the classic blanched almonds add a different flavor to toffee. Honey adds a special quality to this toffee because it is more flavorful than syrup.

MAKES ABOUT 50 PIECES

⅓ cup (2½ oz/75 g) Demerara or dark brown sugar

⅓ cup (3 oz/90 g) granulated sugar

⅔ cup (5 fl oz/160 ml) honey

¼ cup (2 fl oz/60 ml) Swedish light syrup or Lyle's Golden Syrup

¾ cup (6 fl oz/180 ml) heavy cream

Grated zest and juice of 1 lemon

⅔ cup (3 oz/90 g) shelled pistachio nuts

Combine all the ingredients, except the nuts, in a saucepan and bring to a boil over medium heat. Continue to cook for 25–35 minutes until the toffee begins to thicken. Stir occasionally so that the mixture doesn't burn and stick to the bottom of the pan.

While the toffee cooks, place 50 1-inch (2.5-cm) paper candy cups on a tray.

When the toffee reaches 255°F (124°C), or hard-ball stage (see page 16 for how to do a cold-water test), remove the pan from the heat.

Chop the nuts and mix them into the toffee. Fill the candy cups using two teaspoons. Leave at room temperature for at least 6 hours to set.

Look for paper candy cups in kitchenware stores and online. If you don't want to use paper cups for the toffee, you can pour it into a bread pan, as in the recipe on page 67.

TOFFEE CUPS *with* SUNFLOWER SEEDS & COCONUT

Why do we always have to make toffee the classic way? For these, I've used somewhat larger cups and added sticks so they become toffee cups. The sunflower seeds and coconut contribute to making these toffees a little different, but fantastically good. Toasting the sunflower seeds intensifies their flavor.

MAKES 30 TOFFEE CUPS

¾ cup (6 oz/185 g) light muscovado or dark brown sugar

¾ cup (8 fl oz/250 ml) Swedish light syrup or Lyle's Golden Syrup

¾ cup (6 fl oz/180 ml) heavy cream

¾ cup (3 oz/90 g) toasted sunflower seeds

⅓ cup (1 oz/90 g) coconut flakes

You can find the sticks at craft shops or well-stocked kitchenware stores; look for the cups at kitchenware stores or online.

Slowly heat the sugar, syrup, and cream in a saucepan. Cook over medium heat for 20–30 minutes, stirring occasionally with a whisk.

When the toffee reaches 255°F (124°C), or hard-ball stage (see page 16 for how to do a cold-water test), remove the pan from the heat. Stir in the sunflower seeds.

Place thirty 1¾-inch (4.5-cm) paper candy cups on a tray. Divide the toffee into the cups using two teaspoons. Let cool for a while.

Insert a stick into each toffee and sprinkle coconut flakes on top. Leave at room temperature for at least 6 hours to set.

TOFFEE BARK *with* ALMONDS & DARK CHOCOLATE

This crispy, firm toffee is amazingly good. It doesn't have any cream and is cooked to a higher temperature than caramel, so it has a very hard consistency—watch your teeth!

MAKES 1 TOFFEE BARK

5 tablespoons (2½ oz/75 g) butter

1 cup (8 oz/250 g) sugar

⅓ cup (3 fl oz/80 ml) Swedish light syrup or Lyle's Golden Syrup

½ cup (2 oz/60 g) toasted slivered almonds

7 oz (220 g) dark chocolate

Melt the butter in a saucepan over low heat. Add the sugar and syrup and cook over medium heat, stirring constantly, until the toffee reaches 293°F (145°C).

Quickly stir in the slivered almonds and spread the toffee out on a rimmed baking sheet lined with parchment paper. Let cool and then let set for 1 hour.

Chop the chocolate and melt or temper it (see pages 16–17).

Break the toffee into pieces and partially dip each piece into the melted chocolate. Leave until the chocolate has set.

These taste like Swedish Daim toffee candies—but homemade!

VIENNA NOUGAT BRITTLE with HAZELNUTS & ALMONDS

Brittle is a perfect gift because it can be wrapped in cellophane and tied with a lovely ribbon. You can present it either as a whole brittle or in pieces. It can be eaten like candy or crushed and used as an ice cream topping or an addition to a dessert.

MAKES 1 BRITTLE

8 oz (250 g) milk chocolate

1½ tablespoons food-grade cocoa butter

1 cup (8 oz/250 g) toasted and skinned hazelnuts

1 cup (4 oz/125 g) plus 1 tablespoon confectioners' sugar

Pinch of sea salt

1¼ cups (5 oz/155 g) toasted slivered almonds

2 oz (60 g) dark chocolate

Chop the milk chocolate and cocoa butter and melt each in a separate bowl in the microwave.

In a food processor, grind the hazelnuts to a fine, oily paste. With the machine running and adding one ingredient at a time, mix in the sugar, melted chocolate, and cocoa butter, then the salt.

Pour the nougat into a bowl and fold in 1 cup (4 oz/125 g) of the toasted slivered almonds with a rubber spatula.

Pour the nougat onto a rimmed baking sheet lined with parchment paper and sprinkle with the remaining ¼ cup (1 oz/30 g) almonds. Leave at room temperature to set.

Break the brittle into pieces. Melt the dark chocolate (see page 16). Drizzle over the brittle and let the chocolate set.

You can find food-grade cocoa butter in natural foods stores or online. If you prefer, temper the chocolate (see page 17).

CHOCOLATE BRITTLE
with CANDIED NUTS

A perfect recipe to make when a sudden urge for something sweet attacks—it's quick to make! If you prefer milk to dark chocolate, just substitute it. I used the nuts I like best with dark chocolate, but, of course, you can choose your favorite nuts instead.

MAKES 1 BRITTLE

¾ cup (6 oz/185 g) sugar

⅓ cup (3 fl oz/80 ml) water

¾ cup (3 oz/90 g) toasted walnuts

¾ cup (3 oz/90 g) toasted and skinned hazelnuts

¾ cup (3 oz/90 g) toasted blanched almonds, preferably Marcona

14 oz (440 g) dark chocolate

Mix the sugar and water in a saucepan and bring to a boil. Cook the sugar syrup until it reaches 302°F (150°C). Pour in the three kinds of nuts and stir vigorously with a wooden spoon until the sugar whitens and the nuts separate from each other.

Quickly remove the pan from the heat and pour the nuts out onto a rimmed baking sheet lined with parchment paper. Leave to cool.

Chop the chocolate and melt or temper it (see pages 16–17). Mix in the nuts. Pour out onto another rimmed baking sheet lined with parchment paper and leave at room temperature to set.

Break the brittle into pieces.

MILK CHOCOLATE BRITTLE with MACADAMIA NUTS & LICORICE

Licorice powder sprinkled over the thin brittle contrasts nicely with the sweet milk chocolate. Macadamias are fantastic nuts and, when toasted, add a maximum of good flavor.

MAKES 1 BRITTLE

⅔ cup (3½ oz/105 g) toasted macadamia nuts

7 oz (220 g) milk chocolate

1 tablespoon licorice powder

Coarsely chop the nuts. Chop the chocolate and melt or temper it (see pages 16–17).

Line a pan about 8 x 8 inches (20 x 20 cm) with parchment paper. Spread the chocolate in the pan. Sprinkle with the licorice powder and macadamia nuts. Leave at room temperature until set.

Break the brittle into pieces.

If you can't find licorice powder (also called granulated licorice) at your local grocery, look online.

WHITE CHOCOLATE BRITTLE
with RED BERRIES & LEMON

I would say that this is a true summer brittle! Red berries, white chocolate, and lemon—could it be more summery? One tip is to use a real zester or a Microplane grater for the lemon zest.

MAKES 1 BRITTLE

²/₃ cup (¹/₃ oz/10 g) freeze-dried raspberries

²/₃ cup (¹/₃ oz/10 g) freeze-dried strawberries, plus a few extra for decoration

¹/₃ cup (2 oz/60 g) dried cranberries

Grated zest of 1 lemon, plus strips of zest for garnish (optional)

12 oz (375 g) white chocolate

Coarsely crush the freeze-dried raspberries and strawberries and mix them with the cranberries and grated lemon zest in a bowl.

Chop the chocolate and melt or temper it (see pages 16–17). Pour into the bowl with the berries and mix until everything is well blended.

Spread the brittle onto a rimmed baking sheet lined with parchment paper. Decorate the brittle with the extra strawberries and, if desired, strips of lemon zest. Leave at room temperature until set.

Break the brittle into pieces.

You can find freeze-dried fruits in specialty foods stores and online.

MILK CHOCOLATE BRITTLE with PEANUT SWIRLS

Peanuts and chocolate are a combo that I never tire of. I love the swirls on this brittle. It's super easy to make, but oh so very good.

MAKES 1 BRITTLE

5 oz (155 g) milk chocolate

1 oz (30 g) white chocolate

2 tablespoons unsalted
    peanut butter

¼ cup (1½ oz/45 g) salted
    peanuts

1 tablespoon toasted slivered
    almonds

Chop the milk chocolate and the white chocolate. Melt or temper each chocolate separately (see pages 16–17).

Spread the milk chocolate in a thin layer on a rimmed baking sheet lined with parchment paper.

Mix the peanut butter with the white chocolate. Flick the mixture onto the milk chocolate with a spoon and then swirl it around with a dinner knife before the milk chocolate sets. Top with the peanuts and toasted slivered almonds. Leave at room temperature to set.

Break the brittle into pieces.

HONEYCOMB
Porous Honey Brittle

This lovely brittle—a porous caramel with a lot of honey—looks like a bee cake. Honeycomb is great to decorate with and is also good added to other desserts. Break the brittle into pieces or crush it and sprinkle over ice cream, for example.

MAKES 1 BRITTLE

¾ cup (6 oz/185 g) sugar

⅓ cup (3 fl oz/80 ml) honey

¼ cup (2 fl oz/60 ml) water

1½ tablespoons baking powder

Heat the sugar, honey, and water in a saucepan until the mixture reaches 293°F (145°C).

Add the baking powder and stir, but be careful because the mixture can bubble up quickly. Spread the brittle onto a rimmed baking sheet lined with parchment paper. Leave at room temperature to set.

Break the brittle into pieces.

Baking powder makes this brittle porous. Don't stir it too much, or the ingredients will mix too thoroughly and the air pockets will disappear.

CHOCOLATE BRITTLE *with* CRUSHED CARAMEL

This is actually one of the book's easiest recipes, although it looks quite complicated in the photo. The brittle can be very hard, so be careful when you eat it. In the Little Confectionery School beginning on page 13, you can read about how sugar changes color as it caramelizes.

MAKES 1 BRITTLE

⅓ cup (3 oz/90 g) sugar

¼ cup (2 fl oz/60 ml) water

5 oz (155 g) dark chocolate

1 oz (30 g) milk chocolate

1 oz (30 g) white chocolate

Mix the sugar and water in a saucepan and bring to a boil. Cook until the sugar syrup reaches 356°F (180°C) and begins to turn golden brown. When it is a little darker than golden brown, remove the saucepan from the heat (see Caramelized Sugar on pages 13–15).

Pour a thin layer of caramel onto a rimmed baking sheet lined with parchment paper. Leave at room temperature for at least 1 hour to set.

Break the brittle into pieces.

Chop the dark chocolate and melt or temper it (see pages 16–17). Spread it out on parchment paper. Top it with a few pieces of brittle and leave the chocolate at room temperature until it is set.

Melt the milk chocolate and the white chocolate separately and then drizzle each over the brittle. Let the chocolate set at room temperature.

Break the brittle into pieces.

DARK CHOCOLATE BRITTLE *with* COFFEE BEANS & PECANS

When I make this brittle in Sweden, I grate tonka beans (pictured at left) over the top as a fruity and spicy flavor enhancer. They are difficult to find in the United States, but can be substituted with ground almonds, if you like. The brittle is equally delicious with a simple topping of ground coffee and pecans.

MAKES 1 BRITTLE OR
15 SMALL CANDIES

¼ cup (2½ oz/75 g)
   coffee beans

7 oz (220 g) dark chocolate

15 toasted pecans

Coarsely grind the coffee beans.

Chop the chocolate and melt or temper it (see pages 16–17). Spread the mixture out onto a rimmed baking sheet lined with parchment paper or pour into small molds set on parchment paper as shown in the photo.

Top with pecans and ground coffee beans. Let the chocolate set.

Break the brittle into pieces or loosen it from the molds if you used them instead.

Use any of your favorite nuts to accent this simple brittle.

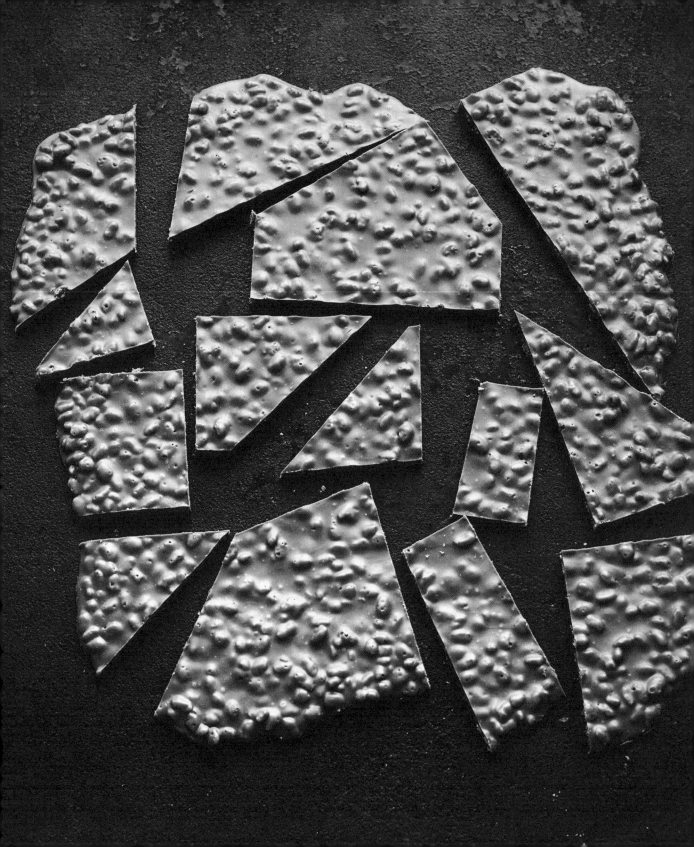

PEANUT CRISP
with MILK CHOCOLATE

This is absolutely the easiest candy to make when you are hit by cravings for both chocolate and peanuts. A simpler version of nougat, it has puffed rice to make it super crispy. Choose a quality chocolate for this brittle.

MAKES 1 BRITTLE

12 oz (375 g) milk chocolate

1¼ cups (12½ oz/390 g) crunchy peanut butter

1½ cups (1 oz/30 g) puffed rice

Melt or temper the chocolate (see pages 16–17). Mix in the peanut butter and stir until the mixture has an even consistency. Fold in the puffed rice.

Line a pan about 8 x 8 inches (20 x 20 cm) with parchment paper. Scrape the peanut butter mixture into the pan and leave at room temperature to set.

Break the brittle into pieces.

CARAMEL SAUCE

All of the sauces in this section can be served warm or cold, but they will taste best either warm or lukewarm. Refrigerate the sauce if you don't use it all right away, then rewarm it over low heat before serving so it will be easy to pour.

MAKES ABOUT 4 SERVINGS

⅓ cup (3 fl oz/80 ml) cream

⅓ cup (3 oz/90 g) sugar

¼ cup (2 fl oz/60 ml) liquid glucose or honey

⅓ cup (3 fl oz/80 ml) water

2 tablespoons butter

Pinch of salt

Quickly bring the cream to a boil in a saucepan. Remove the pan from the heat and set aside.

Mix the sugar, glucose, and water in a saucepan and bring to a boil over medium heat. Cook until the syrup is somewhat darker than golden brown and reaches 365°F (185°C); see Caramelized Sugar on pages 13–15.

Pour the cream into the caramel, one-half at a time, stirring between each addition. Bring back to a boil. Add the butter and salt and stir until the butter has melted.

This sauce is best when served lukewarm over ice cream.

Watch the caramel carefully. It darkens quickly once it starts to brown.

CARAMEL FUDGE SAUCE

I love caramel sauce! This caramel fudge sauce has a slightly thicker consistency and is excellent for desserts with ice cream by itself or ice cream served with fresh berries.

MAKES ABOUT 4 SERVINGS

5 tablespoons (2½ oz/75 g) butter

½ vanilla bean

⅓ cup (3 fl oz/80 ml) heavy cream

¾ cup (6 oz/185 g) plus 1 tablespoon sugar

¼ cup (2 fl oz/60 ml) water

Melt the butter in a saucepan and then cook until it turns golden brown and smells nutty (see Brown Butter, page 13). Stir constantly so the butter won't burn on the bottom of the pan.

Cut the vanilla bean in half lengthwise and scrape the seeds out into the saucepan. Add the cream, bring back to a boil, and then remove from heat.

Mix the sugar and water in another saucepan and bring to a boil. Cook until the syrup is slightly darker than golden brown (see Caramelized Sugar on pages 13–15). One-third at a time, pour in the caramel, stirring well after each addition. Bring back to a boil and then remove from heat.

Serve this sauce lukewarm.

CHOCOLATE SAUCE

Chocolate sauce is a big favorite with me, and I love to eat it with ice cream and meringues. It is one of the easiest sauces to make. I always add the butter last for a rounder flavor.

MAKES ABOUT 4 SERVINGS

1 cup (8 fl oz/250 ml) water

²/₃ cup (5 oz/155 g) sugar

²/₃ cup (2 oz/60 g) unsweetened cocoa powder

¼ cup (2 oz/60 g) butter

Mix ⅓ cup (3 fl oz/80 ml) of the water with the sugar in a saucepan. Bring the mixture to a boil and cook until the caramel is a dark golden brown (see Caramelized Sugar on pages 13–15). One-third at a time, pour in the remaining ²/₃ cup (5 fl oz/160 ml) water. Stir between each addition and then bring back to a boil.

Stir in the cocoa and cook on medium heat for about 5 minutes. Remove from the heat and add the butter. Stir until the butter has melted; let cool.

Serve this sauce lukewarm.

LEMON CARAMEL SAUCE

If you prefer desserts that are a little tart, this is the perfect caramel sauce to drizzle over ice cream or sorbet. The lemon flavor in the sauce goes well with any sorbet, but is especially good with raspberry or strawberry sorbet.

MAKES ABOUT 4 SERVINGS

1¹/₃ cups (11 oz/345 g) plus
   1 tablespoon sugar

²/₃ cup (5 fl oz/160 ml) water

Grated zest of 1 lemon

¹/₃ cup (3 fl oz/80 ml) fresh
   squeezed lemon juice

Mix the sugar with ¹/₃ cup (3 fl oz/80 ml) of the water and bring to a boil. Cook to a light golden brown (see Caramelized Sugar, pages 13–15).

Mix the lemon zest and juice with the remaining ¹/₃ cup (3 fl oz/80 ml) water. One-third at a time, pour the mixture into the caramel, stirring between each addition. Cook on medium heat for about 10 minutes, until the caramel thickens a little. Remove from the heat and strain out the lemon zest using a fine-mesh sieve, if you like.

Serve this sauce at room temperature.

SALTED LICORICE SAUCE

This is the perfect sauce for those times when you are tired of chocolate and caramel. Substitute it for the chocolate in a cream-filled meringue topped with raspberries instead of bananas, and you have a fantastic twist on the dessert. Licorice sauce can also be used to top chocolate cake or torte.

MAKES ABOUT 4 SERVINGS

1/3 cup (3 fl oz/80 ml) licorice syrup

2 teaspoons licorice powder

3/4 cup (6 fl oz/180 ml) water

1/3 cup (3 oz/90 g) sugar

1 teaspoon fine salt

Mix all the ingredients in a saucepan and bring to a low boil over medium heat; cook for about 20 minutes. When the sauce has thickened slightly, it is ready. Remove the pan from the heat and let the sauce cool.

Serve this sauce at room temperature.

Index

Acknowledgments

THANK YOU TO

MY NEAREST AND DEAREST for always being there for me.

GRANDMOTHER, I know you are proud of me!

ANNA, EVA, HELÉN, AND JONNA for a fantastic job—it has been such a pleasure to make this book with you.

ALL THE COLLEAGUES who have inspired me every day.

WERNER'S GOURMET SERVICE for your fantastic products.

weldon**owen**

Published in North America by Weldon Owen, Inc.
1045 Sansome Street, Suite 100
San Francisco, CA 94111
www.weldonowen.com

Weldon Owen is a division of Bonnier Publishing.

COPYRIGHT © Sara Aasum Hultberg 2015
Originally published as *Kola, Fudge, Knäck & Bräck*
First published in Sweden in 2015 by Bonnier Fakta

ENGLISH TRANSLATION Carol Huebscher Rhoades

Library of Congress Cataloging in Publication data is available.

THIS EDITION PRINTED IN 2016

10 9 8 7 6 5 4 3 2 1

ISBN 13: 978-1-68188-117-1
ISBN 10: 1-68188-117-9

PRINTED AND BOUND IN LATVIA